Duck is hungry.

"Yum," says Duck. "A big, fat nut."
Duck eats all the nuts.

Duck is still hungry.

"Yum," says Duck. "A big, fat fish."
Duck eats the fish.

Duck is still hungry.

"Yum," says Duck. "Watermelon!"

"That's my watermelon!" says Hen.

"But I'm hungry," says Duck.

"I'll cut some for you," says Hen.
"Friends share!"